LEVEL 1 SCIENCE
LET'S READ AND FIND OUT

MY FIVE SENSES

BY ALIKI

HARPER

An Imprint of HarperCollinsPublishers

for my sister, Helen Lambros

The Let's-Read-and-Find-Out Science book series was originated by Dr. Franklyn M. Branley, Astronomer Emeritus and former Chairman of the American Museum of Natural History–Hayden Planetarium, and was formerly co-edited by him and Dr. Roma Gans, Professor Emeritus of Childhood Education, Teachers College, Columbia University. Text and illustrations for each of the books in the series are checked for accuracy by an expert in the relevant field. For more information about Let's-Read-and-Find-Out Science books, write to HarperCollins Children's Books, 195 Broadway, New York, NY 10007, or visit our website at www.letsreadandfindout.com.

Let's Read-and-Find-Out Science® is a trademark of HarperCollins Publishers.

Library of Congress Cataloging-in-Publication Data
Aliki.
    My five senses.
    (Let's-read-and-find-out science.   Stage 1)
    Summary: A simple presentation of the five senses, demonstrating some ways we use them.
    ISBN 978-0-06-238191-0 (trade bdg.)—ISBN 978-0-06-238192-7 (pbk.)
    1. Senses and sensation—Juvenile literature. [1. Senses and sensation.] I. Title. II. Series.
QP434.A43   1989   88-35350
612'.8

21 PC 20

Revised edition, 2015

MY FIVE SENSES

I see	I hear	I taste	I smell	I touch

I can see! I see with my eyes.

I can hear! I hear with my ears.

I can smell! I smell with my nose.

I can taste! I taste with my tongue.

11

I can touch! I touch with my fingers.

I do all this with my senses.
I have five senses.

When I see the sun or a frog

or my baby sister,

I use my sense of sight. I am seeing.

When I hear a drum or a fire engine
or a bird,
I use my sense of hearing.
I am hearing.

When I smell soap or a pine tree
or cookies just out of the oven,
I use my sense of smell.
I am smelling.

When I drink my milk
and eat my food,
I use my sense of taste.
I am tasting.

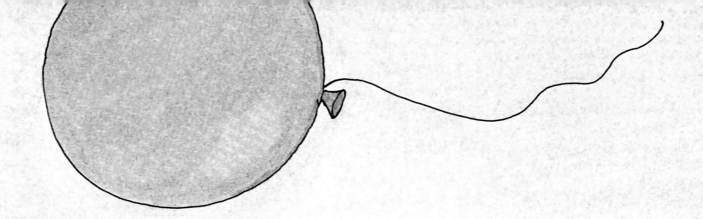

When I touch a kitten or a balloon or water,

I use my sense of touch.

I am touching.

Sometimes I use all my senses at once.

Sometimes I use only one.

I often play a game with myself.

I guess how many senses I am using at that time.

When I look at the moon and the stars,

I use one sense.

I am seeing.

When I laugh and play with my puppy,
I use four senses.
I see, hear, smell, and touch.

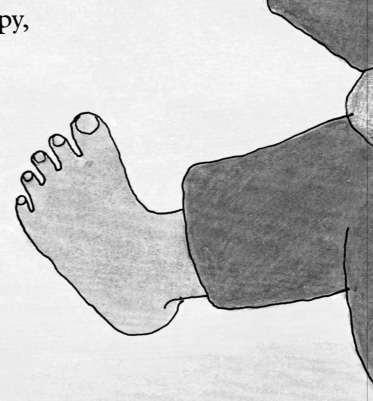

When I bounce a ball, I use three senses.
I see, hear, touch.

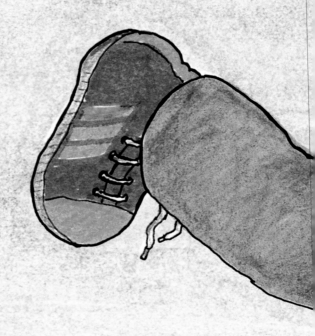

Sometimes I use more of one sense
and less of another.
But each sense is very important to me,
because it makes me aware.

To be aware is to see all there is to see...

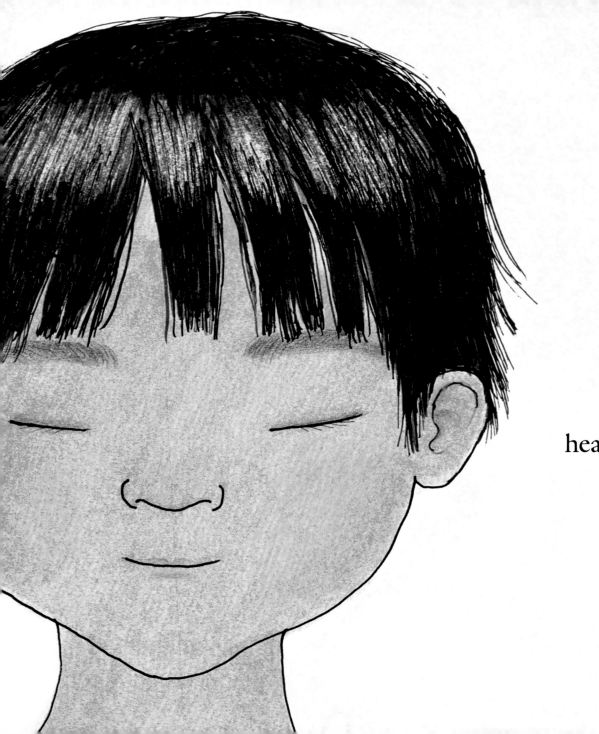

hear all there is to hear...

smell all there is to smell…

taste all there is to taste...

touch all there is to touch.

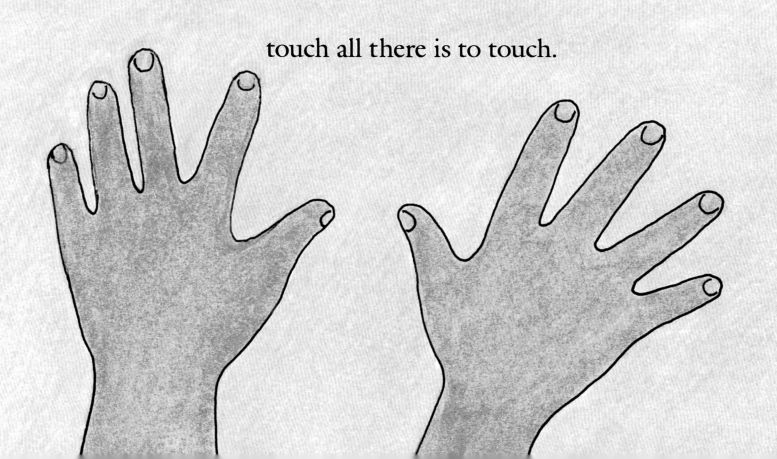

Wherever I go, whatever I do,
every minute of the day,
my senses are working.

They make me aware.